Lessons For Life

Navigating The Course
For Victorious Living

By

Dr. Eddie Jernagin

Lessons For Life

Navigating The Course For Victorious Living

By

Dr. Eddie Jernagin

Copyright @ 2014
All Rights Reserved
Printed in The United States of America

Published By:

ABM Publications

A division of Andrew Bills Ministries Inc.
PO Box 6811
Orange, CA 92863

www.abmpublications.com

ISBN: 978-1-931820-18-9

DEDICATION

This book is lovingly dedicated to my lovely wife,
Mamie Elizabeth Jernagin,
who has been my faithful companion
and my closest friend for many years.

TABLE OF CONTENTS

PREFACE

"Lessons for Life are a compilation of positive life enhancing practical lessons that Dr. Eddie Jernagin has shared with thousands in his fifty years of expounding the gospel of Jesus Christ across America and seven continents of the world.

Messages of faith and truth are vital for successful Christian living. Biblical truth is the hallmark for overcoming various vices we are daily confronted with as Christians in our quest to live free from the deceptive entrapments that seek to captivate and enslave the human spirit.

It is biblically stated that, **"ye shall know the truth and the truth shall make you free."** (John 8:32) Freedom is an inherent right ordained by God. Unfortunately we often allow ourselves to become enslaved to negative thought, ungodly enticements, and destructive allurements.

It is the authors desire that those who choose to read "Lessons for Life" be greatly blessed because of the truth Dr. Eddie Jernagin endeavors to make explicit thereby contributing to your daily quest for maintaining freedom and victory in your desire to live free from the bondages that seek to enslave and stop your positive progress towards spiritual perfection.

Dr. Eddie Jernagin

INTRODUCTION

Each morning when I awaken from a night of restful slumber it is generally my customary routine to greet the Lord in prayerful communion by offering thanksgiving for allowing me to behold the blessed gift of another sun rise and the dawning of a new day.

To behold each morning the rising splendor of the glowing sun, and to breathe the fresh breath of life, knowing it is the Masters generous expression of abounding grace creates within my innermost being a grateful love for life and it's abundant noble opportunities!

Every morning I have the wonderful privilege to glance through the dining room window of our families living quarters to behold the awe inspiring beauty of the majestic Southern California San Gabriel Mountains.

As I walk out the door each day to the outside atmosphere I am often greeted by the melodious singing of birds and the bustling activities of squirrels and other fascinating creatures of God's marvelous creation!

Being blessed to live near the beautiful expanse of Angeles National Forest I often have the honor to see the beauty of Mother Nature and marvel at the Masters creation called planet earth that he has granted for mankind to subdue and enjoy.

There has always been an insatiable desire burning within my innermost being to live forever! Even as a child I often prayed for God to allow me to live forever and never die. In those spiritual immature days of my youth I had little knowledge of the scripture that states, **For as in Adam all die...**" (1 Corinthians 15:22)

It is indeed a fact of reality beyond debate that as long as the Lord prolongs the advent of His "second coming" we who continue to live and pursue chronological longevity will eventually expire with the passage of seconds, minutes, hours, days, months, and years.

The perpetual revolution of "time" takes its toll upon all living matter. Beyond the boarders of "time" however, there exist the God given promise of eternal life! To authenticate this promise Jesus came to planet earth and established the pattern of the kind of lifestyle we must live if we are to personally experience the hope and dream of eternal life in the ultimate sense of infinity.

My prayer as a child to live forever is actually possible because of Jesus who did no sin. Christ survived a string of events that would have defeated most men of lesser character and strength. Jesus survived cataclysmic evil confrontations by the love he had that was stronger than death that he also had to overcome.

Now that Jesus has successfully overcome death my dream and desire as a child to live forever is an attainable reality not only for me but to all those who will accept Jesus as their personal Lord and Savior!

"So in Christ shall all be made alive! (1Corinthians 15:22)

CHAPTER 1

ORDER MY STEPS

Temporal life is one of the most complex experiences you will ever have to deal with during your earthly life span. I choose to use the word "temporal" because there is a temporal season as well as an eternal season of human existence. Human kind is eternal because we are created after the God Kind! Unfortunately, we are eternally lost creatures if we fail to adhere to God's counsel.

What an individual does in his or her temporal season of life will greatly influence their eternal destiny. It is of utmost importance therefore for mankind to develop a disciplined life style to Gods Divine plan for our life if we expect to experience a blissful eternity. Life is like a complex maze. To get through it successfully depends upon submissiveness to Gods righteous counsel.

We are often prone to rely on our carnal instincts to get us through simple and complex situations, only to end up in frustration due to our unwise decision making. Or we fall victim to the "something told me syndrome" rather than wisely evaluating that "something" by Gods counsel (the written Word of God).

Following Divine biblical direction will always get you through no matter what the obstacles are that are working against you. God's word will always accomplish its purpose. It is based upon His omnipotent supernatural authority!

The question is asked in Romans 8:35, **"Who shall separate us from the love of God?"** There are always evil forces opposing the Lords righteousness for your life. It is important to be acutely aware of God's love and the Supreme price that has been paid by Jesus for our ultimate success over all opposing forces.

The Apostle Paul wrote in Romans 8:31…..**"If God be for us, who can be against us."** The Lord can use the most unlikely sources to deliver us when we are following his navigation to get us through our challenging experiences. We must at all times trust him to order our steps. (See Proverbs 3:5).

The Psalmist David reminds us of God's divine guidance as he relates the following: **"The steps of a good man are ordered by the Lord: and he delighteth in his way. "Thou he fall, he shall not**

be utterly cast down, for the Lord upholdeth him with his hand." (Psalms 37:23-24) The preceding text reflects the importance of being obedient and disciplined to following God's navigation.

The pleasure of the Lord in your actions of following his directions equips you for success no matter how severe the staggering odds. If God is upholding you it is virtually impossible for you to fail. The hand of the Creator is the Supreme hand of power!

Much too often we have a human tendency to wrestle with the Lord ordering our steps because we can not see the ending from the beginning. Or our lack of faith allows flesh and carnality to dictate our course of action.

Be reminded however, that Joseph who was sold by his brothers into Egyptian captivity became the sacrificial object for his family as God in his divine providence gave Joseph favor with his captives.

The evil that had been perpetrated for Joseph's demise became the saving grace for his family to be sustained during the famine that had confronted Joseph's kindred and countrymen.

When your steps are being ordered by the Master you should never permit adversity to conquer your mental stability and overcome your confidence in the Almighty's Supernatural ability to supersede satanic strategy. Always be reminded that when your steps are being ordered by Divine Providence, God is in control. Allow his miraculous manifestation to do what he has devised to lead you to astounding victory!

The Supreme Wisdom of The Almighty is never subjugated to error! He always sees the ending from the beginning! As the old saying reminds us, "While you are trying to figure it our, God has already worked it out!" Trust Him and lean not unto your own carnal reasoning!

CHAPTER 2

CONSTRUCTIVE LEADERSHIP

When one speaks of leadership it implicates a high profile position. A good leader must have a vivid visionary perception. You cannot ethically and efficiently lead others to constructive objectivity without having cohesive imagery or basic frame work as the basis for noble projects and beneficial goals.

If you are to be an effective leader you must remember that others under you are following your plan of operation. The bible reminds us that, **"Without a vision the people perish. "Where there is no vision the people perish."** (Proverbs 29:18) Also it reminds us that, **"If the blind lead the blind they both shall fall in the ditch."** (Matthew 15:14)

The church is the most important institution on the earth, because it is dealing not just with politics or secular matters but with the souls of human beings! It is therefore paramount for leaders within the "Body of Christ" to develop and dedicate themselves to high spiritual quality leadership skills that will influence and perpetuate

17

the pursuit of positive and worthwhile goals. The leader must know what they want to accomplish and also be able to precisely convey the vision to the group or team they are leading.

Pastors have urgent need for lay leaders in the church to help facilitate and accomplish the vision that God has given for ministry outreach. Pastors are anointed to shepherd the body of believers they have been given the Divine charge to oversee and lead. But, pastors are not anointed to do everything themselves independent of a team. Without a team to assist in the accomplishing of the goal burn out would be imminent. That is why the team (body ministry concept) is necessary within the church to help the vision come to fruition.

Jesus Christ chose twelve disciples who went through the process of training and refinement to help perpetuate the kingdom of God in the earth. We get a glimpse of the team concept as we see it being established in the New Testament Church (See Acts 6:1-7). Here we see a biblical pattern of sub-divisions of leaders and workers under the direction of the Holy Spirit as tasks have been assigned to persons within the church to complement the overall structure and vision of reaching the masses and attending to inner administrative church needs. The team concept also helped to lighten the burden and load encountered by the chief elders and balanced the load of the overall operation of the New Testament Church.

The most effective leader is not always one who seems to possess the charisma and savvy that breeds popularity. We have but to look at those who were divinely called and appointed to positions of leadership to establish this fact.

The following personalities listed establishes this reality: (1) Moses: A sheepherder, not eloquent of speech when commissioned by God to stand before Egyptian royalty to demand the release of the children of Israel out of captivity. (2) Apostle Paul: Had a speech impediment but became a great apostle and prolific writer of New Testament scripture. (3) Peter: An uneducated fisherman with character flaws who endeared himself to Christ and became a great disciple, preacher, apostle, and great soul winner. Through obedience and dedication to the divine call to leadership these ordinary men became extra ordinary leaders used by an awesome God!

A spiritual leader must have the following qualities to assure spiritual success: (1) Divine call and ordination by God to carry out the Divine assignment. (2) Obedience and willingness to say yes to The Divine call no matter what the challenge or sacrifice. (3) Vision: Divine plan and insight for accomplishing the goal to be achieved. (4) Faith: The belief in the Divine call and willingness to step out on God's orders. (5) Prayer: Staying in daily communication with the Lord for daily direction.

The following represents thoughts for leaders to ponder: (1) Your worth and stability as a spiritual leader is brought to surface as a result of oppositional confrontation. (2) How you as a leader handle problems will affect the outcome of your projected objectives. (3) Antagonistic forces are a necessary evil to evaluate the strength, resolve, and nobility of your leadership. (4) Your ability to solve problems makes you an effective and valuable leader worthy of respect of those you lead. (5) Whether there are two or 1,000 in your group problems will inevitably arise.

Every individuals obedience to the Divine call to leadership will be judged by God who has called you! Strive with all your heart to fulfill your calling in a way that is pleasing not for the accolades of men, but for God's glory!

CHAPTER 3

SPIRITUALITY

What does it mean to be spiritual? This is an important question that deserves a clear explanation. Too often in some religious circles it is expressed in an emotional display of speaking in unknown tongues, prophetic discourse, or mystic manifestations. This is not to imply that these are erroneous concepts. But we often are guilty of overlooking spirituality in a more paradoxical simplistic yet very powerful dimension.

In a simplistic basic sense being spiritual can be defined as one's connection to God by faith and their ability to function with supernatural authenticity at His direction. It is very important that we should be aware of true spirituality as well as superficial deceptive spirituality.

The world and the church should be aware that deceptive spirituality is a prevalent danger that exist in society on a massive scale. It is demonic in its essence and very contagious especially for those who seek to be "super spiritual" or those void of the capacity to discern the rudiments of deception.

Christ warned us about the objective of satanic aspirations when he said, **"The thief cometh not, but for to steal, and to kill, and to destroy..."** (St. John 10:10).

We must be alert that deceptive spirits are at work even in the midst of the church to imitate genuine spirituality and counteract against God's manifestation of righteousness.

Authentic spirituality has its rudiments deeply imbedded in the Creator and was made manifest in Jesus Christ the Son of God and the things he did during his in person earthly ministry. Jesus explicitly stated when he was physically on earth these important words: **"My food is to finish the work that he gave me to do."**

Notice in the preceding text that Christ was completely focused on the will of God for his mission in ministry. He also stated in St. Luke 4:18-19 the following: **"The Spirit of the Lord is upon me, because he hath anointed me to preach the gospel to the poor, he hath sent me to heal the brokenhearted, to preach deliverance to the captives, and recovering of sight to the blind, to set at liberty them that are bruised. To preach the acceptable year of the Lord."** (KJV Holy Bible).

From the preceding text we see that spirituality is involved in bringing deliverance to human needs. It is an active God given prowess to do something about the adverse conditions all around us. Not just going to church every Sunday and being content and comfortable with that alone.

Spirituality is active at correcting societal ills because we have been spiritually qualified by the Holy Spirit to do so!

A prime example of deceptive spirituality was resident in Lucifer, the archangel who originally inhabited of all places heaven! Lucifer was in the midst of the heavenly inhabitants knowing the power of authentic spirituality, yet scheming to preside in the position of Supreme dominance!

The following discourse reveals Lucifer's motivation of deceitful spiritual pride and also his disgraceful fall: **"How art thou fallen from heaven, O Lucifer, son of the morning! How art thou cut down to the ground, which didst weaken the nations!**

"For thou hast said in thine heart, I will ascend into heaven, I will exalt my throne above the

stars of God: I will sit also upon the mount of the congregation, in the sides of the north.

"I will exalt my throne above the stars of God: I will sit also upon the mount of the congregation, in the sides of the north.

"I will ascend above the heights of the cloud; I will be like the most High.
"Yet thou shall be brought down to hell, to the sides of the pit." (Isaiah 14:12-5).

Lucifer's fall should remind us of how dangerous it is for anyone to permit pride and selfish motivation to go beyond the boundaries of God's intended purpose of one's gifting. It will not only lead to the gifted person's downfall.

It can likewise mess up the lives of others who are weak and vulnerable to such deceptive practices.

I have personally witnessed in my fifty four years of ministry all too many individuals fall victim to demonic spirituality especially when it comes to the gifts of prophesy, working of miracles, and discernment of spirits. Not to imply that these are not authentic spiritual gifts. However, for the love of money these gifts are often emulated and misused to gain monetary compensation from weak and desperate victims who seek quick fixes and are willing to pay for a so-called word in their desperate attempts to acquire deliverance or quick solutions to their circumstances.

There is danger in equating spirituality solely by religious emotion, mystical manifestations, spiritual readings, so called prophesy, incoherent utterances, etc. These may indeed be associated with spiritual implications.

We must be aware nevertheless, that there is such a things as demonic spiritual association. The King of Tire is referenced in scripture as the **"anointed cherub."** (See Ezekiel 28:14). He abused the privilege of access he had to the anointing.

We have but to look at Jesus Christ to get a vivid example of true spirituality. It is seen in his humility of character, love for humanity healing the sick, casting out evil spirits, forgiving sinners, feeding the hungry, patience longsuffering, man of prayer, and performing everything he was call of the Heavenly Father to do! It is unfortunate that these simple unique characteristics are often overlooked as vital connections to genuine spirituality.

If in our life's quest we seek to adhere to the pattern that Christ established on earth as an obedient servant to the Father's will spirituality will become ultimately perfected.

Sometimes redundancy is necessary for the sake of retention and genuine spirituality has to do with disciplined consistent practice of feeding the hungry, clothing the naked, doing good to those who you know may not like you. Being spiritual is that of forgiving your offender, "turning the cheek", going the extra mile. Also, loving and being compassionate, enduring evil, patient, visiting the sick. I could go on and on, but I think you get the picture!

If in any of these categories of spirituality you find yourself coming short of the mark. You should honestly admit and repent of such short fall before the Lord. After confession and repentance we then would be wise to learn from the experience of King David after having fallen short of God's righteousness. He repented and then vowed to do something positive to make up for his shortcomings. (See Psalms Chapter 51).

CHAPTER 4

Developing Spiritual Character

The greatest contributing factor for problems on the earth can be summed up in one word — rebellion! This self condemning sin is ingrained in fallen nature stemming from the ancestral of Adam and Eve who rebelled against God in the Garden of Eden.

It does not matter how undefiled the outer surface of the human façade may appear. All according to the Word of God "have sin and come short of the glory of God." (Romans 3:23)

Throughout history we see the warfare of good and evil factions clashing in human nature. And the wretchedness of sin defying the purity of God's glory in everything God has created. And perhaps some are prone to wonder why it is that evil seems to have such a stronghold on such a massive scale.

It was not in the heart of the Creator to create homosapien robots having no choice of free will. Rather it was in the sovereign will of our Maker to give his human masterpiece the power of choice.

How very tragic it is that we all too frequently utilize our free will to do wrong things. Consequently, our character becomes adversely contaminated with vain and vile activity that motivates us to do ungodly things.

The Apostle Paul who was plagued with this vain lifestyle of sinful wretchedness prior to Christian conversion discovered a life changing solution to the sinful captivity to do evil before he was converted to Christianity. Herein he discovered the God-Kind of lifestyle.

An examination of the following text gives us an example of Paul's sinful dilemma and his ultimate solution to the character problem:
"So I have learned this rule: When I want to do good, evil is there with me. In my mind I am happy with God's law. But I see another law working in my body. That law makes me war against the law that my mind accepts. That other law working in my body is the law of sin, and that law makes me it's prisoner. What a miserable person I am! Who will save me from this body that brings me death? I thank God for his salvation through Jesus Christ our Lord! So in my mind I am a slave to God's law, but in my sinful self I am a slave to the law of sin. (Romans 7:21-25) Holy Bible-Easy to read version)

Sanctification or giving of one's life over to the Christian life becomes the key to the development of Good Christian character. Until this is achieved we can not overcome the carnal actions of the fallen Adamic nature.

The following is a list of common carnal strongholds identified as attributes of contaminated character listed in Galatians 5:19-21:

*Adultery: Voluntary sexual intercourse between a married person and any other than the lawful spouse. *Fornication: Voluntary sexual intercourse on the part of an unmarried person with a person of the opposite sex. *Unclean: Not clean, dirty, morally impure, evil, vile. *Lasciviousness: Inclined to lust. *Idolatry: The worship of idols. Blind adoration, reverence. *Emulations: Desire or ambition to be equal or surpass. *Wrath: Intense anger, rage, any act carried out in great anger for punishment or vengeance. *Strife: The act or state of fighting or quarreling, contention. *Seditions: Rebellion, stirring up discontent against the government in power. *Murder: The unlawful and malicious or premeditated killing of one human being by another. *Drunkenness: Intoxicated or habitually intoxicated. *Revelings: To glory in rebellion, resisting authority.

It would be a travesty of immeasurable proportions if the negatives of Adamic nature were permitted to govern the life of humanity. But God through the infinite power of his incomparable grace has liberally given the Fruit of His Spirit that we may overcome the works of the sinful flesh. The following attributes can be found in Galatians 5:22-23 and are listed below:

*Love: An act of compassion and grace beyond measure and without reservations. *Joy: Overwhelming exuberance of pleasure and inner elation. *Peace: A blissful state of inner calmness regardless of the severity of boisterous situations. *Longsuffering: The spiritual ability to face and endure prolonged adversity without self destructing. *Gentleness: The act of entreating confronting situations with calmness and concern without harsh and erratic emotion or heavy handedness. *Goodness: Rendering unto others benevolent service without expecting reciprocation of the same. *Faith: An abounding confidence and trust in obedience to and acting upon God's instructions without reservation. *Meekness: Mild mannered disposition not easily provoked and kind. *Temperance: Balanced dispositions, self-restraint in conduct.

If the preceding attributes are the practicing principles and quality of your character a reflection of Christ is resident. And that becomes a living testimony of how wonderful it is to be a Christian. Others may also be drawn to Christ by what they observe of him in your demeanor!

CHAPTER 5

THE DIVINE CALL TO MINISTRY

"One day as Jesus was walking along the shore beside the Sea of Galilee, he saw two brothers-Simon, also called Peter, and Andrew fishing with a net, for they were commercial fisherman.

"Jesus called out to them, "come, be my disciples, and I will show you how to fish for people!

"And they left their nets at once and went with him.

"A little farther up the shore he saw two other brothers, and John, sitting in a boat with their father, Zebedee, mending their nets. And he called them to come, too.

"They immediately followed him, leaving the boat and their father behind.

"Jesus traveled throughout Galilee teaching in the synagogues, preaching everywhere the Good News about the Kingdom. And he healed people who had every kind of sickness and disease.

"News about him spread far beyond the borders of Galilee so that the sick were soon coming to be healed from as far away as Syria. And whatever their illness and pain, or if they were possessed by demons, or were epileptics, or were paralyzed-he healed them all.

"Large crowds followed him wherever he went-people from Galilee, the Ten Towns, Jerusalem, from all over Judea, and from east of the Jordan River." (Matthew 4:18-25) (New Living Translation)

The preceding reference reveals a vivid portrait of the highest order of servitude. We do indeed see the result of Jesus Christ fulfilling the Divine Call to ministry!

~IT'S NOT ABOUT TITLES~

Contrary to general thought I believe a minister does not have to carry an ecclesiastical title to fulfill his or her ministerial assignment. An effective minister however, must be a dedicated servant with a sincere undefiled motive of serving God as he serves others. If and when he does with consistent efficiency his ecclesiastical title becomes apparent regardless of verbal pronouncement.

When Jesus met the Samaritan woman at the well his discourse was so profound and revelatory until his prophetic office became clearly noticeable. And the Samaritan woman could not help but to notice and say, **"I perceive that thou art a prophet!"** (St. John 4:19)

In my early tenure as a young traveling evangelist I was occasionally asked if I was a prophet, I usually responded to that question by saying, "my ministry speaks for itself!"

Much too often there is such a tendency to get so caught up in our ministerial title more so than fulfilling the challenging service of our title and position. We who are called by God are what we are because Gods anointing resides upon our life and not just the title we may have acquired!

The call to ministry is a call to the most important positions of service one could ever experience. This is so because it is a call dealing with the eternal destiny of human souls. We are called not for the sake of obtaining a title but for the cause of bringing deliverance, hope, and salvation to fallen humanity.

IT'S NOT ABOUT MONEY!

Undefiled ministry that is ordained by God requires the called individual to walk by faith!

If a minister does what he or she is supposed to do by giving and providing faithful and effective service their just rewards are inevitable and benefits will come to them.

It never ceases to amaze me how that in these contemporary times when we ask some of our more prominent ministers of our day to render their ministerial services that one of the first things they want to know is how many members do you have, or are you willing to give me a designated financial honorarium to come to you.

True ministry is a walk of faith! Jesus told his disciples to, **"carry neither purse, nor script, nor shoes, and whosoever house ye enter, first say, peace be to this house."** (Luke 10:4) It is quite apparent that we have long sense the time of the inception of the New Testament apostles and disciples drifted away from this mode of serving!

Less we forget we must never turn down an assignment or invitation to minister because the crowd is small or for the lack of financial compensation. We do well to remember that out of all the multiplied millions on the face of the earth God took time out of his busy schedule to personally visit and save you and I on a one to one personal basis! Neither has he ever ask us for financial compensation for his abundant services.

There is one amazing thing about the divine call by God. The Lord often calls the most unlikely people to accomplish his purpose. A diligent search of scripture reveal that the calling of God of servants for ministry were men who would not rank among the elite when it came to genius. Rather, he often called uneducated and ordinary low profiled men. Ironically, when those ordinary men were converted and endowed with the holy ghost they became extraordinary servants bringing hope, healing and the message of deliverance that made a profound impact upon the multitudes!

MINISTRY TESTING

Ministry is often put to various testing by circumstances and situations we would rather avoid. Consequently, there are some necessary evils that ministers and ministries must encounter for the sake of strength and development and enhancement of the anointing we must have for effective ministry.

In the book of St. Luke chapter four we observe the ministry of Jesus being put to the test in preparation for development of ministry confrontation. Keep in mind that there would be no need for ministry if everything was indeed perfect. To the contrary ministry must always concern itself with problems that need to be solved.

I have witnessed countless times persons who started out with zeal on assignments they thought God had assigned rather that having absolute knowledge of the fact. It is very important to know as opposed to guessing at your assignment.

I recall the story of a young aspiring evangelist who excitedly told his pastor that the Lord had called him to the evangelistic field. With vigor he pursued the course of evangelizing. After a few tough experiences while he was on the field he encountered some rough sledding. He soon returned back to his home church with less vigor and enthusiasm than what he started out with.

When asked by his pastor about his lack of enthusiasm about evangelizing, he responded to his pastor that God changed his mind and said "never mind!"

We must keep in mind the reason God calls us to fulfill an assignment is because needs exist in life and you with the backing of the Lord are able to fulfill the mission! There is an old wise saying that states, "whom God calls he qualifies!"

True ministry will inevitably require a need for renewal of spiritual strength. The more you give of your ministerial service refueling is necessary for future assignments!

"But they that wait upon the Lord shall renew their strength; they shall mount up with wings as eagles; they shall run, and not be weary; and they shall walk and not faint. (Isaiah 40:31)

CHAPTER 6

AGENTS OF CHANGE

In the midst of all things that are good that God has created, mankind heads the list of the crowning achievement of Gods master plan of creation.

The Psalmist King David was so awe struck by the magnitude of man's superior quality above all creation that he was inspired to write a Psalm expressing his wonderment of this fact:

"When I consider thy heavens, the work of thy fingers, the moon and the stars, which thou hast ordained:

"What is man, that thou art mindful of him? And the son of man, that thou visitest him?

"For thou hast made him a little lower than the angels, and hast crowned him with glory and honor.

"Thou madest him to have dominion over the works of thy hands: thou hast put all things under his feet:

"All sheep and oxen, yea, and the beast of the field;

"The fowl of the air, and the fish of the sea, and whatsoever passeth through the paths of the earth!" (Psalms 8:3-9)

When one reflect on the preceding scripture with intense meditation and observe the contemporary condition of man's diminished and contaminated character in light of his "god likeness," perhaps you cannot help but possibly wonder how could we have fallen so far from the grace of God in whose image we are to represent?! The simple answer is of course, disobedience!

To correct this cataclysmal flaw in the human race God came to earth in the likeness of sinful flesh in the person of Jesus Christ as an agent of change to bring a solution for human kind's fallen state of being.

When the dispensation of grace under the New Covenant beheld Jesus they saw first hand a "new breed" of human kind coming to bring a righteous change to a sin cursed world! Emanuel (God with us) who was able to overcome and excel over temptation and the challenge of demonic forces!

(See Romans 5:19). Christ came bringing a life-changing "Kingdom of Heaven" message of salvation, healing, and deliverance. Not only did he bring this "kingdom of heaven message" of hope, but also his personal lifestyle exemplified that of the kingdom message he taught.

If this contemporary generation and generations of the future are to effectively promote the gospel message of change, the evidence of this change must be resident and vividly seen in us by those who walk in darkness. If you are going to talk the talk, you must likewise walk the walk! (See Luke 4:18-21)

We in this 21st Century live in a time of history when there is increased knowledge and a grasp of understanding and learning theological precepts more than any other previous generation. But our carnal mode of living contradicts the change we so often profess in our preaching and teaching.

It was Jesus who said, "If I be lifted up I will draw all men unto me." Agents of change must practice what they preach and teach. Positive change must be reflected within the character of the messenger. Because professing and not possessing genuine Christian deliverance projects hypocrisy.

On a very noteworthy occasion in Jesus' earthly ministry he was teaching in the temple a message of hope and change when in walked the scribes and Pharisees who brought unto him a woman taken in adultery. And when they had set her in their midst they challenged Jesus as to whether she should be stoned according to the Law of Moses. Their interest and concern was more caught up in the legalisms of the law more than sharing with the woman a message of repentance, forgiveness, love and change. When Jesus detected their motive he challenged them by saying, **"He that is without sin among you, let him first cast a stone at her."** (John 8:7) We who profess to be agents of change must search our own heart before sharing the message of change lest we be also guilty of sin just as the person we are trying to get delivered!

The empowerment of believers with the Holy Ghost equips the Body of Christ to initiate and bring about change in our society. However, if we neglect to fulfill our mission as agents of change many souls may suffer when we neglect our mission.

The baptism of the Holy Ghost is not intended to be hoarded to one's personal appeasement, rather it is to be shared with compassion to saving and rescuing lost mankind from the vice of sin, sickness, and death that too many souls among us are experiencing!

We have been issued by God the keys to the kingdom of heaven to initiate positive change on the earth. Take notice of the following scripture text: **"And I will give unto thee the keys of the kingdom of heaven: and whatsoever thou shalt loose on earth shall be loosed in heaven."** (Matthew 16:19). What a supreme gift of authority the Heavenly Father has given to the church to bring about miraculous change on the earth!

The New Testament church was given unparalleled authenticity on the day of Pentecost to perpetuate astounding spiritual and physical transformation in the world! This torch of spiritual fire has been passed on to this generation. The Apostle Peter said it with spiritual fervor, **"For the promise is unto you, and to your children, and to all that are afar off, even as many as the Lord our God shall call."** (Acts 2:39)

The modern day church has a great responsibility to continue the ministerial legacy of Christ who is the very foundation of the churches operation. If believers fail to continue what Christ our Founder has established the life of many will suffer enormous eternal loss!

CHAPTER 7

BUILDING A CHURCH THAT GLORIFIES GOD

The birth of the Christian church as seen in the book of The Acts of the Apostles reveal a panoramic view of the church as it multiplied daily in building a viable body of believers to the glorification of God. This important progressive movement set the stage for the contemporary church to immolate.

Building a church that glorifies the Lord is vital to the authenticity of baptized believers who profess being connected to Jesus Christ. Our Lord and Savior Christ Jesus is the solidified foundation on which the Christian church establishment and effective operation is dependent upon.

The term, "building a church" implies that the continued growth of the church is a perpetual process that must transpire until Christ returns for his bride (the church) and say's "well done!"

Jesus' inquisition as to his identity among the populous that we read of in the book of Matthew chapter 16, was profoundly answered by the Apostle Peter who was a disciple of Christ when he replied, **"thou art the Christ son of the living God."**

To be a church that glorifies God the character of the church must inevitably reflect that of Jesus who is the "author and finisher" of the churches faith!

Much too often we are prone to get overly excited by glorifying the numbers of our mega churches membership roster while overlooking the important fact that building our churches to glorify the Lord must deal more specifically with the sanctification quality of each member rather than numerical quantity only and financial abundance!

Bulging numbers do not always reflect sanctification quality that profiles Jesus' character. However, let's face it, we should definitely be concerned about multiplying the number of souls we persuade to accept Jesus Christ as their Lord and Savior!

What we do with the number of souls that join our church congregations as disciples is of utmost importance. The sanctified or Christian church must teach the church body the importance for each member to practice daily the moral principles of holiness that will cause God to be glorified in our life style as we walk in the midst of society.

The glorified church must be the church that not only talks the talk of holiness, but one who walks the walk of her infallible foundation, Jesus Christ!

The church that glorifies God must know how to utilize the spiritual keys she has been given by Christ. The following scripture excerpt expresses this invaluable gift: **"And I will give unto thee the keys of the kingdom of heaven: and whatsoever thou shalt bind on earth shall be bound in heaven: and whatsoever thou shall loose on earth shall be loosed in heaven.** (Matthew 16:19)

The preceding biblical reference exposes us to a gift that when utilized by faith will produce deliverance that will demonstrate to the world the glorification of God within the church thereby bringing conviction of God's glory to a sinful society.

God's power working through you and me as Christian believers introduces our glorified God to skeptics by bringing conviction of their need for Him in their lives!

If the contemporary church is to glorify the Lord our congregations must be infused with the "Christ anointing" (Spiritual infusion of power that qualifies one to do what Jesus did.) Operating under the authority of this incomparable spiritual force will ignite positive change in the earth!

The church, representing the Body Of Christ, must not be so caught up and preoccupied in having the glorification of ecclesiastical titles i.e., Bishop, Apostle, Prophet, Prophetess etc., that we overlook the paramount fortification of having the anointing that works independent of our positional titles! If the Lord manifested his power to utilize such animals and instruments as a donkey, a rooster, a rod, and an axe head that floated on water, certainly he can use you regardless of having or not having an impressive ministerial or ecclesiastical title!!!

It bears repeating that a church that glorifies God is one that is doing what Christ did! God was so pleased with Jesus until he verbalized his pleasure. **"This is my beloved son in whom I am well pleased! (2 Peter 1:17)**

If you are a professing Christian is God being glorified by the things you do and say on a daily basis? Are their positive works being performed as a result of your confession of Christian faith? Are others being persuaded to come to Christ for Christian conversion as a result of his character being reflected by the things you do and say? If so you are helping to build the church that glorifies our Lord and Savior Jesus Christ!

Chapter 8

KINGDOM CITIZENS

The most unique personality of human kind to ever inhabit planet earth is that of Jesus Christ of Nazareth. His immaculate conception defied the biological trend of nature. And his brief tenure of physically living on earth for a period of thirty three short years produced more good than that of Methuselah who lived on earth as a human entity for nine hundred sixty nine expansive years!

Jesus' unique position of being both God and man defies logical human explanation! His persona was of such nature that even the intelligence and wisdom of sages could never surmount or parallel. They too, were captivated and awe struck at the awesome display of the Saviors astounding demeanor under unparalleled pressure.

Humanity without a doubt witnessed a "new breed" of human-kind as it marveled at Jesus' wisdom, his simple yet powerful teaching, and his superb discipline. His coming to earth ushered in a unique kingdom age never witnessed before in the annals of history. John the Baptist announced his coming to earth with a message urging repentance form sin and the Adamic way of living. Although John was a unique and popular figure in his own unique forerunner position, he was quick to proclaim in his message to the populace that he was unworthy to even unloose his (Jesus') sandal strap! (See John 1:27)

The unique kingdom that Christ bought to earth unlike the kingdoms of carnal and corrupt potentates was infused with such spiritual characteristics of Divine origin until those who today will submit to the infallible teachings of Christ are ushered into a new life style reflective of Christ himself. Thereby qualifying them as "kingdom citizens" of heaven on earth!

This unique citizenry is referenced in scripture as one having **"righteousness and peace, and joy in the Holy Ghost."** (Romans 14:17)

As a kingdom citizen those who are Saints on earth have the capacity to influence their space in a positive manner no matter where they may roam! The exposure and observation of the sanctified life style of kingdom citizens reveal to the world of fallen humanity that the spirit of Christ is resident within their being. This in turn becomes a tremendous witnessing reservoir displaying the eternal value and beauty of Holy Living based upon the personality of Jesus Christ.

All kingdom citizens may not be able to sing like an angel or even preach like Paul the Apostle. However, the life practice and character of a kingdom citizen displays to fallen man the value and beauty of aligning one's life with the "God Kind" of victorious sanctified living in the midst of a sin infected society!

Kingdom citizens (Christians) have been given spiritual keys to effect positive change in the earth. In the book of Matthew chapter sixteen we learn that these spiritual keys are necessary spiritual empowerment made available to kingdom citizens to operate in a similitude of Christ who is the foundation of the Christian Church.

We of the Christian church who represent Christ on the earth have been given awesome spiritual authority and power to effect and bring about positive change in this troubled and sinful world. The Lord expects and demands productive Christian service from his chosen vessels to go forth among lost mankind bringing about positive manifestations among human populous! These are the last of the last days. Whatever we do for

the up building of the Kingdom of God in the earth
we must do it now!

CHAPTER 9

ABOUNDING GRACE

What is grace? It is the unmerited expression of abundant love and mercy that has it's origin in the heart of God that he unselfishly shares with all human kind without expecting compensation in return for it's value!

~A DREAM COME TRUE~

I am always at awe when reading the biblical account of the creation of the universe and the incomparable beauty that is innate within its glorious existence. All of this as a result of a dream becoming true that was in the heart of God. Just to know that God had within his heart to create the earth and then turn the helm over to man to subdue and control the beautiful contents makes the story of the creation even more remarkable!

God as the soul creator did not hoard his vast creation but graciously and unselfishly created god-like offspring to supervise the miraculous wonder of it's unique treasures. From the inception of creation until now we experience the act of abounding grace being manifested from the spirit of God towards all who populate the human family.

Grace is not something that we earn as a result of monetary exchange. Neither can it be obtained by an act of any tangible object. Rather, authentic grace operates as a unique gift from the heart never expecting a favor in exchange for the monumental services it provides. In fact the Lords grace is invaluable and can never be assessed! It is eternal due to the fact that it comes from the eternal God!

~GOD KIND OF LOVE~

"For God so loved the world, that he gave his only begotten Son, that whosoever believeth in him should not perish, but have everlasting life. (St. John 3:16)

The preceding scripture reveal an act of grace that reflects the unique and unselfish nature of the grace of the Lord. "...God so loved..." I like the little word "so" because it adds to the enormous unique gesture of compassionate mercies and grace. "So love." It is a love beyond the norm. It is emphatic, and filled with measureless giving! Jehovah's love is a graceful act of giving to "all" without prejudice! God so loved that he gave. Ask yourself the question what am I sharing? The love that I profess to have is it the "God-kind" of Love? Is it the love that keeps on giving regardless to what it receives in return? Is it the kind of love that reflects God's abounding grace that lives within me due to my confession of Christ within me!?

~FROM DEATH TO LIFE~

"For since by man came death, by man came also the resurrection of the dead.

"For as in Adam all die, even so in Christ shall all be made alive." (1 Corinthians 15:21-22)

Due to the sin of Adam and Eve who were progenitors of the human race death became the consequence for all Adamic offspring. There disobedient actions actually challenged the abounding grace of Almighty God!

Death that was never intended to be for the demise of mankind became a devastating reality! One might ask the question, how could it be known that death for man was never intended to be? It is based on the fact that God is eternal, and man was created in Gods image and death was, and death is not a characteristic of the eternal

God image! God is God and always will be God Eternal and death is not a characteristic of Gods eternal being!

~DEATH AND SIN vs ABOUNDING GRACE

"...But where sin abounded, <u>grace did much more abound.</u>" (Romans 5:20) Thank God for abounding grace for it is stronger and overrules death for those who choose to repent of sin and accept the gift of eternal life in Christ,
who is Gods abounding and gracious answer to the human need!

Because of sin infiltrating the human race as the result of Adams fall the death experience is a common occurrence among us. Thanks be to the act of grace Christ in the life of all who accepts eternal life from him will supersede the eternal curse of death. For death is only temporary for the redeemed. Due to the gift of grace however, the redeemed in Christ will live eternally! Sin and death is indeed no match for abounding grace!

~ULTIMATE ACT OF GRACE~

"For when we were yet without strength, in due time **Christ died for the ungodly**.

"For scarcely for a righteous man will one die: yet peradventure for a good man some would even dare to die.

"But God commendeth his love toward us in that, while we were yet sinners, Christ died for us. (Romans 5:6-8)

Sin is totally offensive to God! Through an ultimate act of his mercy and grace towards humanity he gave his sinless son to become sin for us and go to a rugged cross and die for our opportunity to be saved from our sins! What an act of incomparable love and mercy expressing the abounding grace of our God. To our God in Christ we now owe an eternal debt of gratitude!!! In Him and by his grace we live, and have our eternal existence. This is the everlasting wonder of Jehovah Gods abounding grace!

CHAPTER 10

MANHOOD/WOMANHOOD

The union of man and woman becoming connected as one sets the stage for the propagation of the human race. The merging together in intimate sexual union fulfills the will of God for the female and male genders to..."Be fruitful, and multiply, and replenish the earth..." (Genesis 1:28)

Man and woman represent the most highly developed primates on the earth. This is true because of their being created by God in the pattern of his likeness and given the divine authority to dominate over all the earth.

It was in the divine providence of God for the male gender to be the first created among the biological genders, male and then female. As a man the male gender is divinely ordained to be in the forefront of headship. Not that the female is of less value, notwithstanding, without both genders coming together in compassionate sexual intimacy procreation would be adversely affected. Man and woman are both powerful in their perspective roles and neither have to compete for supremacy.

The headship of a father is an awesome responsibility that requires proper character development that is vital to the nurturing of the human family. A father's character is reflected in his paternal attitude towards his wife and their offspring as well as life in general.

~A FATHERS LOVE~

The most profound emotion humanity can ever express and experience is love. This unique virtue permeates the divine person of God our heavenly father who is the total epitome of its authentication. The genuine love of a devoted God loving father enhances the cohesiveness and joy of livelihood for the male, his female companion and his entire family household. A father who does not share genuine love and affection with his family deprives his wife and siblings a true image of noble headship!

One might ask the question, "how can a father's love be best expressed?" It is profoundly expressed by setting the example of a father who has accepted God's answer to the human need,

Jesus Christ! It is expressed with a father who prays for and with his family on a consistent basis!

A father who accepts Christ is one whose character reflects an exemplification of compassion, patience, and willingness to sacrifice for the sake of his families overall safety and spiritual well being. A loving Christian father leads by righteous example as he teaches his family Christian principles and allows his family to see firsthand those same attributes operating in his own lifestyle on a daily basis!

~JOB~

The image portrayed in the life of the biblical personality by the name of Job, illustrates a profound display of leadership and love of a devoted father. The following profiles the well rounded character of Job as a dedicated father: (1) He dedicated himself in worship and service to God (2) He respected God and avoided evil (3) He and his wife produced a fruitful offspring of ten children (4) He was financially sound (5) He loved his family and (6) He was a prayerful intercessor for his family. (See Job 1:1-5)

God our Heavenly Father and creator epitomizes the foremost image of a loving father.

We see this love being gestured to all humanity in his insurmountable generosity **"...For God so loved the world that he gave his only begotten son that whosoever believeth in him should not perish but have everlasting life."** (St. John 3:16)

A God fearing father is willing to make the ultimate sacrifice for his family. This can be accomplished by his faith and allegiance to God. His reliance upon the Lords strength to sustain he and his family stabilizes his emotions in the midst of all opposing odds that may confront he and his family! Having an **"I can do all things through Christ who strengthens me"** mentality stabilizes a "God fearing" fathers positive stance to withstand the odds!

~MOTHERHOOD~

Unique power is innate within the realm of motherhood. Without it the reproduction of life would be non-existent. God has sanctioned the biological process of reproduction of the human race by the establishment of motherhood as well as fatherhood.

The female gender is unique in that women are biologically constructed to bear the gender of human species. I like to call it the "tabernacle" of human offspring. God undoubtedly knew that the male gender could never bear the load of child birth. Also, the sovereignty of God has so ordained for a woman to bear children.

With motherhood comes the awesome responsibility of nurturing her biological offspring and setting the pace of righteous living for her offspring to immolate her high moral character. When I speak of high moral character I speak of that character that is resident in Jesus Christ. Christ prayed for all of humanity and set the pace of true love and true devotion to the will of God. A true woman of authentic Christian motherhood must practice righteous maternal devotion to her children and submissive loyalty to her spouse. A mother must pray for her family and live a life of holiness before them to practice in their life's tenure.

~PATERNAL HEROES~

No one should be more of a hero in the life of a child than the child's parents. Much too often children look to outside family sources for a hero figure. Both mother and father must spend quality time in the life of their offspring. Not only sending them to church, but going to church faithfully with the entire family! Mothers and fathers in our modern society are often guilty of sending their children to our ungodly secular schools on a daily basis! But, when it comes to their consistence of sending them to Sunday school or positive church activities fall short of the mark of consistency!

There is an old wise saying that states, "a family that prays together is a family that stays together." When there is a consistent coming together as a family in prayer it affects the moral standard of the family in a beneficial way. Manhood plus Womanhood coming together in the oneness of a loving and prayerful relationship equals replenishing the earth with fruitful human offspring!!

CHAPTER 11

DIVISING A CHRISTIAN MARKETING STRATEGY

"Go ye therefore, and teach all nations, baptizing them in the name of the Father, and of the Son, and of the Holy Ghost:

"Teaching them to observe all things whatsoever I have commanded you; and, lo, I am with you always, even unto the end of the world. Amen." (Matthew 28:19-20)

It is of paramount importance before you put together any marketing program in reference to Christian outreach that God be acknowledged prior to your attempt to put it into operation. It is always tempting to adopt secular and corporate ideas because they seem to be successful. However, it is important to keep in mind that the Lords church is run by the Holy Spirit and not by intellectual pursuits.

Looking in retrospect to centuries of the past as well as contemporary times life reveals the continuous quest of mankind's effort to survive the ever pressing activities of life. The Christian church consisting of converted disciples of Christ has been commanded by God to universally reach the masses with the salvation message of the gospel of Jesus Christ.

Not only have we been spiritually endowed by God for effective ministry; we the church of Jesus Christ must devise constructive programs and strategies to effect spiritual growth and development within our local and international congregations.

Whatever means we utilize to reach the masses we must keep in mind that the message of the gospel must never be compromised to appease sinful customs and varied philosophies of the ungodly in secular society. The methods and means however, may vary due to geographical locations or media availability, etc.

It should be consistently stressed and thoroughly understood by the church body that every Christian is a member of the marketing team! We have but to look at the New Testament church to see how proficiently the church was when they had all things common and willing to share unselfishly with the local and far reaching communities what they had received as a result of being filled with the Holy Spirit.

One of the greatest marketing tools that the church has that is one of the chief ingredients of the Holy Spirit is "love." This chief attribute of the Holy Spirit was exemplified in immense measure in the life of Christ. It became the foundational basis for the greatest marketing attribute of all times. Every marketing tool to be effective must be motivated by this supreme attribute.

If a viable universal marketing strategy is to be initiated the local church must play the lead roll of educating their parishioners as to the importance of Kingdom Building.

~MARKETING DEFINED~

In a general sense marketing is the act of buying or selling in the market place items you deem worthy of purchase.

Marketing defined from the Christian perspective is that of sharing on the universal stage of life Christianity as the ultimate life style base upon the free gift of Jesus Christ to all of human creation with the objective of winning the world from the damnation of sin to the saving grace of Jesus Christ!

~MARKETING RESERVOIRS~

The ways and means of marketing the gospel are numerous. Modern technology provides the church with multiple ways to share and market the gospel as never before in the history of the Christian Church. Jesus Christ, the greatest human to ever inhabit the earth was immensely prophetic when he stated, **"Verily, verily, I say unto you, He that believeth on me, the works that I do shall he do also; and greater works than these shall he do; because I go unto my father." (John 14:12)**

The following represent effective marketing tools: (1) Personal testimonies of conversion one on one (2) Preaching and teaching (3) Tract distribution (4) Radio, Television, internet (5) Bible distribution, Christian book publication (6) National and international revival campaigns (7) Food and clothing ministry (8) Out door street services (9) Door to door witnessing (10) Home bible study etc.

~CHRISTIAN EDUCATION CLASSES~

Before there is a launching of evangelism on an international scale there is no place for forming the basis in preparation for foreign fields like the home front. The following information represents a comprehensive approach to "Christian

Education" that will contribute to preparing committed Christian disciples in preparation for spearheading and marketing world wide evangelism:

Christian education is a vital link to the organizational structure of the church. Once people have experienced conversion, it is important that they be exposed to consistent Christian education that is conductive to their continued spiritual growth and development. Not only is this vital for new converts but equally as vital to those who have an experienced walk with Christ. Christian education in this dispensation must address the needs of the whole man as we endeavor to increase the moral standards of society. The challenge is very great however, it is one that can be achieved as we professing Christians dedicate to the cause!

~BASIC CURRICULUM OBJECTIVE~

(1) To introduce biblical principals that contributes to the development of Christian character within the life of the believer. (2 Corinthians 5:17)

(2) To equip ministries with the tools for constructive church development and

ideals that will produce effectiveness. (See Ephesians 4:11)

(3)   Display the image of Christ within our lifestyles. (See Philippians 2:5)

(4)   To transform man's reality so that God can create in him a Divine greatness (See Romans 12:2)

(5)   To authenticate the affect of the church in societal development. (Matthew 5:13-16)

~WHOLE NEEDS CONCEPT~

It is important that the whole needs concept for ministry be taught within the local church so that an effective marketing outreach encompasses the importance of meeting the whole need of humanity. This vital concept is vividly seen in the narrative of St. Luke 4:18-19. The following is a brief exegesis of the concept:

I.   **THE ANOINTING:** Authentic endowment and qualification for divine service.

II.   **THE POOR:** Spiritual and physical depravity due to ignorance and unsatisfactorily nourished.

III.   **THE BROKEN-HEARTED:** Wounded by the issues and challenges of life that can only be rectified by the divine touch of the master.

IV. **DELIVERANCE TO THE CAPTIVES:** Spiritual and physical detainment against the will that defies the basic right of freedom and the call of Christians to freedom in him.

V. **SIGHT TO THE BLIND:** Conditions of inept ability to visualize Christ and his lordship because of visual impairment due to blindness in the natural and spiritual realms.

VI. **LIBERATION:** Conditions of deep emotional hurt caused by confrontational experiences in relationships and bitter altercations. Entrapped by personal pains that has caused considerable detachment and withdrawal from society and condition of psychological imprisonment of mind.

VII. **THE ACCEPTABLE YEAR OF THE LORD:** Past, present, and future seasons of deliverance for the entire human race!

It is imperative that every church ministry maintain maximum consistency in church growth and an explicit competent ministry development program. The purpose, plan and procedure are all very vital to the edification of your ministry. The following elements will increase the unity of the faith between each member and thereby promote kingdom growth on a universal scale.

OUR SALVATION:
(1) Belief
(2) Confession
(3) Baptism
(4) Communion (1 Corinthians 11:24-26)

OUR STATEMENTS:
(1) Our purpose statement: Why we exist.
(2) Our vision: What we intend to do.
(3) Our faith statement: What we believe
(4) Our value statement: What we practice.

OUR STRATEGY:
(1) Brief history of your church.
(2) Ministry target market.
(3) Strategy to meet needs.

LOCAL CHURCH STRUCTURE
(1) Organizational flow chart.
(2) Church association vision.
(3) Quarterly leadership meetings.

~DEFINING COMPONENTS FOR EFFECTIVE CHURCH GROWTH~

"And they continued steadfastly in the apostles doctrine and fellowship, and in breaking of bread, and in prayers.

"And fear came upon every soul: and many wonders and signs were done by the apostles.

"And all that believed were together, and had all things common;

"And sold their possessions and goods, and parted them to all men, as every man had need.

"And they, continuing daily with one accord in the temple, and breaking bread from house to house, did eat their meat and gladness and singleness of heart,

"Praising God, and having favor with all the people. And the Lord added to the church daily such as should be saved." (Acts 2:42-47)

From the unity of the church we see exemplified in the preceding scriptural passage key offices of ministry service for edifying the church body and marketing the gospel.

Church ministry is the lifeblood and circulatory system

of the organizational structure of the church. Ministry provides the church with a vehicle by which the body can remain fitly joined together. The church school curriculum should include a comprehensive course study on the following four basic ministries as seen in (Ephesians 4:11-12) (1) The ministry of the Apostles (2) The ministry of the Prophet (3) The Ministry of the Evangelist (4) The ministry of the Teachers (5) The ministry of the Pastor.

~EXPLICIT EXPOSURE~

The visionary leader of the church will eliminate a great deal of misunderstanding and confusion among the congregational body if he establishes an educational curriculum that presents in clarity the directions in which the church has been divinely instructed to pursue.

There should be for all ministry participants a clear recognition of individual giftedness and calling for specific service in ministry; and all support leadership must be taught to have a shared passion for the vision and the strategies by which goals may be achieved. All ministry workers should be united in knowledge, perception and procedure through consistent training. This will facilitate strong church cohesion!

~CULTURE AWARENESS~

When we look at the issue of ministry we must realize that the call of the church is to minister on a worldwide scale. The church marketing vision must not be void of cross culture inclusiveness.

It is important to research and study the customs, needs, and culture of those areas of the world that you intend to share ministry.

Paul wisely reminds us of the importance of the adaptability to be inclusive to sharing the gospel with all men universally in the following excerpt:

"For though I be free from all men, yet have I made myself servant unto all, that I might gain the more.

"And unto the Jews I became as a Jew that I might gain the Jews: to them that are under the law, as under the law, that I might gain them that are under the law;

"To them that are without law, as without law, (being not without law to God, but under the law to Christ) that I might gain them that are without law.

"To the weak became I as weak, that I might gain the weak: I am made all things to all men, that I might by means save some.

"And this I do for the gospel's sake, that I might be partaker thereof with you." (1 Corinthians 9:19-23)

It is not necessary to have years of exposure to many years of Christian experience before you can qualify to market or share with others about Christ. There are various biblical accounts in the New Testament where new converts were very effective in sharing their positive life changing experience of accepting Christ as Savior.

One's personal testimony of Christian conversion can often be effective in marketing what you have personally experienced as a result of newly being "born again." (See Acts 9:17-22)

~DEVELOPING STRONG LEADERS~

An efficient market strategy must take under consideration the need for strong leadership to lead the way for those who are a part of the marketing personnel. Leaders are called and ordained for the purpose of sound spiritual leadership.

Ironically when it come to calling men or women to the helm of good leadership God can call some of the most unlikely people. However, the so called ordinary people become extraordinary when Holy Spirit endowed!

~LEADERSHIP PERSONALITY~

For leadership success in the marketing program the three areas of the personality of the leader are undeniable essential for leadership success: (1) **CONVICTION-** The leader must have a conviction concerning that in which he is involved, without wavering. (2) **CONSTRAINMENT-** This element leads to the staying power of the leader. There is an inescapable affect that the knowledge of God's love and power presents. (3) **COMMITMENT-** This element derives from the aforementioned elements. The leader cannot arrive at this provisional essential if he does not first enter through the gates of conviction.

The development of spiritual discipline and keen sensitivity to God's guidance and not your own carnal self-serving ideas is vital to group marketing success. Efficient spiritual leadership is based upon divine direction rather than upon natural or scholastic aptitude. (1) Trusting the divine source not human instincts. (2)

Preparation, determination and consecration will help produce proper development. (3) We must recognize that time and space are two major contributions to mature leadership development and marketing strategy.

It is very important that one carefully consider the cost of the awesome task of leadership. Even so, in counting up the cost, a full assessment of leadership position can only be attained through first-hand experience. The following are some basic areas to consider: (1) Personal sacrifice (2) Spiritual submission (3) The challenge of isolation (4) The challenge of delegation.

If after reading the information you have just concluded and are interested in receiving additional information you may order additional information by requesting:

"Devising a Comprehensive Christian Marketing Strategy for Local and Universal Outreach"

Dr. Eddie Jernagin
New Dimension International Ministries
PO Box 976
Muncie, IN 47308

CHAPTER 12

EVIL IS GOOD??

"And out of the ground made the Lord God to grow every tree that is pleasant to the sight, and good for food; the tree of life also in the midst of the garden, and the tree of knowledge of <u>good and evil</u>."

"I form the light, and create darkness: <u>I make peace, and create evil:</u> I the Lord do all these things." (Genesis 2:9)

One can see no good in "evil" unless you can comprehend it from a Christian perspective and what it causes a true dedicated children to gain from its confrontation. Ironically, for the true Christian it brings out the best rather than evil for evil and eventual defeat! Paul the Apostle said it very well when he stated, **"all things work together for good to them that love God, to them who are the called according to his purpose."** (Romans 8:28)

When a committed Christian truly loves the Lord he or she will follow the pattern of Jesus who always defeated evil by letting his light shine thereby exposing evil for the negative of its intensions. However, the evil that is spoken of in reference to Gods making has a positive reasoning for being rather than a vile evil objective!

The following is a brief excerpt taken from the Doctor of Philosophy Dissertation written by yours truly (Bishop Eddie Jernagin) in 2012, in reference to the subject matter entitled, **"The Paradoxical Conclusion of Evil As it Relates to the Christian, Evil is Good."** I trust that it will bring out your best Christian attributes as a result of your own personal battles with evil confrontations!

~Evil is Good As it Relates to Biblical Characters/Lamb of God~

~Joseph~

A most intriguing exposition recorded in the book of Genesis revealing that "evil is good" is seen in the life experience of Joseph who was the youngest of eleven male siblings whose father was Jacob. Joseph was loved by his father more than any of his other children because he was the son of Jacob's old age.

Jealousy is often the envious vice that will surface when favoritism is seen in family relationships. Josephs' brother hated him because of their father's unparalleled love for him.

Jealousy can become a very dangerous weapon when it is allowed to fester and motivate the jealous individual to employ evil impositions towards the object of their target. This became the case in the life of Joseph's older brothers when a dream that Joseph had was conveyed to them. The dream which revealed subservience of the older siblings to the younger Joseph became more than they could bear. The very thought of servitude of the older brothers to the younger was reason enough for the older brothers to devise an evil plan for their brother's destruction. The vile plan ultimately led to Joseph being sold into Egyptian slavery and physical imprisonment.

The bondage of enslavement is immensely degrading and robs one of freedom and human dignity. Homosapiens are created in the image of God to be free moral agents divinely exempted from the imposed vice of involuntary evil servitude. Human slavery projects the portrait of one human being as superior to his fellow human-kind.

The evil gesture of family rejection that Joseph's brothers were guilty of committing would undoubtedly be more than the average individual would be able to endure. However, whenever the Divine plan of God is being manifested, evil that is permitted towards God's chosen will ultimately work in favor of the just!

The Divine mind of God can never be fully understood by mere human intellect. This would certainly be true in Joseph's case. The following biblical text gives credence to God's supernatural mind:

"For my thoughts are not your thoughts, neither are your ways my ways, saith the Lord.

"For as the heavens are higher than the earth, so are my ways higher than your ways, and my thoughts than your thoughts." (Isaiah 55:8-9)

All of the negative experiences Joseph had to endure were ironically by Divine design that ultimately blessed not only Joseph and his family, but his fellow countrymen as well.

The Divine providential strategy was detrimental to satanic strategy in that the cataclysmic adversity Joseph had to endure proved to work for the good of all who were involved in the entire scenario. The ironic paradox of evil schemes produced "abundant good" in the final analysis to the glory of God!

Joseph's journey from the pit to the kings palace and eventually to the governmental position as Overseer of a foreign land (Egypt) speaks volumes to the paradoxical assertion that "evil is good" when God is in the plan!

~Job~

Life is a complex experience that requires much intellectual and spiritual stamina to endure its multiplicity of challenges. Within the Hebrew Bible, the book of Job relates the fascinating story of the biblical figure by the name of Job. He was indeed a unique and strong individual who withstood more adversity than most men could ever endure.

Job was totally devoted and dedicated in his relationship with God. He was also an immensely wealthy individual who never allowed the reality of his monetary and carnal possessions to supersede his daily prayer devotion and allegiance to God. In fact, the scriptures describe Job as one who "...**was perfect and upright, and one that feared (reverenced) God, and eschewed (avoided) evil.**" (Job 1:1)

There transpired a day in the life of Job when Satan challenged God to allow him to take away Jobs blessings as a test to jobs faith and devotion. Soon Job is desolate, covered with boils, his wealth is diminished and his family dead. Three friends arrive to comfort him; he disputes with them, denying he had done anything to deserve such a plight. In spite of the entire dilemma, Jobs faith is undaunted! At the end of all the cataclysmic evils and Jobs confrontation with God, the power and mystery of the deity are memorably reasserted, but the problem of why the innocent suffer is left unsolved.

The evil pressures Job had to confront eventually drove him to curse the day he was born but he never cursed God who by divine design allowed the negative confrontations to transpire.

Imagine the Jubilation that must have permeated Satan's spirit when Job cursed the day he was born after the intense pressure he was experiencing seemingly became more than what he thought he could bear.

However, little did the adversary realize that all the cataclysmic negatives were working for Jobs **"good"** beyond his ability to discern.

As Bishop W.R. Portee, one of my wise spiritual mentors said, "The more adverse circumstances I experience in my life as a Christian minister, the more relaxed I become." Of course as a young inexperienced understudy at that point in my ministerial experiences, I was unable to comprehend the logic of that statement. However, in my ministerial maturation Bishop Portee's statement became clear.

Its meaning is simply this: "The more battles you overcome with the help of God, the more you know that your current trying circumstance shall pass with you being the victor and not the victim." The Lord has a perfect record of success and will always have the last say!

After all the tough cataclysmic battles that Job had to endure in his painful scenario in the final analysis, his faithfulness was rewarded, and he won the war! The following biblical excerpt attest to his success:

"So the Lord blessed the latter end of Job more than his beginning: for he had fourteen thousand sheep, and six thousand camels, and a thousand yoke of oxen, and a thousand she asses.

"He had also seven sons and three daughters. "And he called the name of the first Jemima; and the name of the second, Kezia; and the name of the third, Kerenhappuch.

"And in all the land were no women found so fair as the daughters of Job: and their father gave them inheritance among brethren.

"After this lived Job as hundred and forty years, and saw his sons, and his sons' and his sons' sons, even four generations.

"So Job died, being old and full of days." (Job 42:12-17)

The victorious conclusion of Job's encounter is a proven paradoxical testimony that "evil is inevitably good" when permitted by God to test the faithful commitment of a dedicated servant!

~APOSTLE PAUL~

Most biblical scholars consider Paul as one of the greatest apostles in the annals of biblical history. A historical profile captures the attention of most bible readers as they read about his unique conversion experience to Christianity. The Apostle Paul's interesting life was filled with challenging adventures that defies the thought that Christianity is a religion of total peaceful tranquility void of pain and suffering. The following biblical excerpt supports this fact:

"The righteous cry, and the Lord heareth, and delivereth them out of all their troubles.

"The Lord is nigh unto them that are of a broken heart; and saveth such as be of a contrite spirit.

"Many are the afflictions of the righteous: but the Lord delivereth him out of them all.

"He keepeth all his bones: not one of them is broken.

"Evil shall slay the wicked, and they that hate the righteous shall be desolate.

"The Lord redeemeth the soul of his servants: and none of them that trust in him shall be desolate." (Psalm 34:17-22)

Suffering for the Lords glory is a realistic phenomenon that is difficult to understand from an intellectual or carnal perspective. It is also difficult at most to comprehend from a spiritual perspective. When one examines the sufferings

Paul encountered after being converted to Christianity, it would be seemingly correct to assume that his sufferings were linked to his reaping what he had sown from persecuting the Saints of God prior to his Christian conversion. However, this was not the case because God is not a God of vengeance once one's sins are forgiven, they are covered by the blood of Jesus without any thoughts of vengeance on the Lords behalf!

Paul in his epistle to the Corinthians (2nd Corinthians 11:23-33) describes his great sufferings. He faced immense physical tortures by way of severe beatings with stripes and rods; receiving a total of 39 stripes from the Jews on five different occasions. Paul faced massive perils everywhere in the world. He was not at all blessed with favorable weather patterns as he sailed on the waters during his confrontational tempestuous fulfillment of ministry. He was consistently confronted by antagonistic opposition. Many times he suffered from hunger and thirst as well as nakedness, weariness and painful circumstances!

Along with his physical sufferings Paul had to care for all the churches and their challenging circumstances. His ministry was not a flamboyant experience as we see many of today's mega ministries. Paul verbalizes his request to the Lord to remove what is described as **"... a thorn in the flesh, the messenger of Satan to buffet me lest I should be exalted above measure."** (2 Corinthians 12)

After accepting divine providence in his challenging experiences in ministry the Apostle Paul ironically rejoices while verbally glorifying the Lords Divine will for his painful confrontations in ministry!

Paul accepted the fact that the Lords grace was sufficient to sustain him regardless of the negatives he had to encounter on his destined course of dedicated ministerial servitude! It is indeed a fact that when you're in the Master's favor regardless of the evil that challenges you, you are in the dominant position which conclusively defends our paradoxical projection that evil as it relates to the steadfast committed Christian is good!

~JESUS CHRIST/LAMB OF GOD~

"He is despised and rejected of men; a man of sorrows, and acquainted with grief: and we esteemed him not.

"Surely he hath borne our grief, and carried our sorrows: yet we did esteem him stricken, smitten of God, and afflicted.

"But he was wounded for our transgressions; he was bruised for our iniquities: the chastisement of our peace was upon him; and with His stripes we are healed." (Isaiah 53:3-5)

Jesus Christ who is God's answer to the human need confronted an unprecedented amount of evil. The gross sins of all humanity were upon his shoulders. The Son of God who committed no transgressions, was made to ironically become sin so that all of humanity could be redeemed from the curse that the evil of sin inflicted. No one but Jesus could ever bear such atrocities of evil and pain and survive victoriously.

It is beyond the comprehension of the wisest sage as to how God could have such profound love for a sinful populace and give his son who knew no sin to die for the redemption of a vile and sinful world! The gross agony Christ experienced is totally beyond description as to the capacity of its evil essence. We can only attempt to describe the measure of the evil and painful debts of its unparalleled happenstance!

If Christ after his encounter with the evil leading to his death had never attained resurrection from the vice of death, the reality of eternal life for the Christian would be beyond attainment! The evil impositions inflicted upon Christ proved to be less powerful and dominating than the abounding good that it paradoxically produced.

Those individuals who choose to align themselves with the Christian belief of eternal life through Christ by accepting Him as Lord and Savior of their lives can also live eternally even after their temporal earthly demise!

The following text expresses the paradox of life after death, all because of what Christ has accomplished after successfully enduring evil and the stronghold of death:

"Behold I show you a mystery; we shall not all sleep, but we shall be changed, In a moment, in the twinkling of an eye, at the last trump; for the trumpet shall sound, and the dead shall be changed.

"For this corruptible must put on incorruption, and this mortal must put on immortality.

"So when this corruptible shall have put on incorruption, and this mortal shall have put on immortality, then shall be brought to pass the saying that is written, Death is swallowed up in victory.

"O DEATH, WHERE IS THY STING? O GRAVE; WHERE IS THY VICTORY." (Corinthians 15:51-55)

One should always be mindful that the agonizing mental and physical sufferings of Christ was a necessary evil experience he suffered to expose evil's degradation in contrast to the "eternal positive good" brought to pass by His humble demeanor through the entire scenario of evil imposition!

Now that Christ has survived over the evil imposition of the crucifixion we who receive him as Lord and Savior now have access to "eternal life" even after our temporal demise. The evil was temporary, the glorious and ironic positive benefits are everlastingly victorious! To God be all the eternal glory!

CHAPTER 13

PRAYERFUL COMMUNICATION

It is impossible to navigate through this complex maze of life without the ability to communicate. The exchange of ideas as well as cohesiveness of ideas leading to a state of oneness in agreement all combine to making effectual communication possible.

Since humanity is Gods idea our bond to him inevitably calls for us to stay in consistent communication with our divine heritage. Neglecting to do so leads to eventual eternal defeat.

Today's society is in a state of cataclysmic confusion due to mankind's failure to follow Gods guidance and also trying to make life successful without his infallible perception. The Word of the Lord emphatically tells us to acknowledge and trust him for direction. (See Proverbs 3:5-6) Jesus Christ also admonishes us in (St. Luke 18:1) that, **"...men ought always to pray, and not to faint."** The consequences for not daily following a disciplined communication pattern with him and not following specific direction all contribute to the lost and confused state of being the world finds itself in today!

I am very fascinated with the navigation system of my cell telephone. I speak into it and tell it where I want to go and it directs my course. When I get off track it directs me how to corrects my course. As accurate as my telephone navigation system appears to be, it can not direct my course through this complex maze called life! This is something that only God can do! Daily communicating with the Lord and totally depending and obeying his guidance leads to ultimate victory and success over all opposing forces!

~QUALITY TIME~

In a book that I have written entitled, **"Communicating with God"** makes reference to the fact that time is a gift freely given to all things that exist in life. The revolution of twenty-four hours accounts for a complete day. This being a fact of life gives us equal and ample opportunity to fulfill our noble purpose.

If we neglect to spend quality time within those twenty-four hours communicating with the Lord we are subject to make wrong decisions in life that can keep us from accomplishing our positive purpose.

Life is issue oriented and man needs a Super Natural Wisdom to supersede that of his own finite intellect. This is why we are encouraged in the scripture to take time to communicate and acknowledge the Lord for daily direction. Count the times you have made wrong choices because of neglecting to spend quality time in the presence of God. If you are honest I am sure those times are too numerous to recall them all.

Spending quality time in prayer not only acquaints you with the Lord, but also teaches you the value of patience and trust in His ability to rightfully direct your course in this complex and challenging life! Making hasty decisions without consulting the Master in prayer can often lead to disastrous consequences.

How much time do we spend in earthly association of idle time with friends, television, and casual communication with others, in comparison to our spending quality time in intimate conversation and visitation of our Creators counsel? Perhaps the comparison is very one-sided in favor of secular activity rather than being with the Lord. It is indeed little wonder that we have made more than our share of wrong decisions!

Discipline is required to spend consistent quality time in prayer. Once you can master this discipline it leads to positive growth and development of personal character. In addition, you will enjoy success that will save you from a lot of pitfalls and entanglements that Satan has devised to entrap you!

I believe that when Jesus was in the Garden of Gethsemane praying prior to His destined crucifixion on the cross, He spent quality time with God seeking fortification to face the experience. This attributed to His being able to deal with the issue of the cross and the agonizing death he was to endure. In that moment of prime time he gained strength to confront the inevitable. He was able to bear the burden because of what he released in prayer to the care of the Father.

Spending quality time in prayer can be challenging because of the adverse tactics of interference. Maybe you have experienced interruption of your prayer time by the ringing of the telephone or your child wanting attention. I have even experienced a knock at the door during my intimate time of communion with the Lord! The examples are truly too numerous to mention! If however, you can press beyond the interference you are bound to enter into the Supernatural! When you reach this pinnacle of spiritual ecstasy the communication becomes a joy, which propels you beyond the reach of outside forces that desire to hinder your prayer connection.

Usually, at this particular juncture, the Holy Spirit has now taken over the prayer and now you began to utter words in worship beyond earthly comprehension because you are now experiencing a spiritual high beyond the enemy forces!

CHAPTER 14

FAITH AND PERSISTENCE

I have chosen to conclude "Lessons For Life" (Navigating The Course For Victorious Living) with a few reflections written from my book, "Fulfilling Your Purpose" published in 1995. It is my belief that every human being is created in Gods image and has a positive purpose to pursue in life. I base my assumption upon the following biblical narrative:

"So God created people in his own image; God patterned them after himself; male and female he created them.

"God blessed them and told them, multiply and fill the earth and subdue it. Be masters over the fish and birds and all the animals.

"And God said, "Look! I have given you the seed-bearing plants throughout the earth and all the fruit trees for your food.

"And I have given all the grasses and other green plants to the animals and birds for their food."

"And so it was. "Then God looked over all he had made, and he saw that it was excellent in every way. This all happened on the sixth day." (Genesis 1:27-31) (Holy Bible-New Living Translation)

Since man is the profile image of God it is imperative that we maintain intimate fellowship and have unshakable trust in his purpose for our being. Faith allies you in spiritual fellowship with Him. It becomes the connecting bond between the Heavenly Father, son and daughter relationship. Without faith according to the scriptures it is impossible to please the Creator! (See Hebrews 11:6)

Any worth while potential you have is deeply embedded in Gods ability working within you. **"For it is God who works in you both to will and to do for his good pleasure."** (Philippians 2:13) Your working in and with his plan for your life produces inevitable success!

~ROSTER OF THE FAITHFUL~

In the book of Hebrews chapter eleven we see the roster of the faithful obtaining a "good report" as they devotedly walked with God by faith: By faith Able; by faith Enoch; by faith; Noah; by faith

Abraham; by faith Isaac; by faith Jacob; by faith Moses; etc. And so, as you can see the biblical patriarchs as well as the apostles and New Testament followers all walked with the Lord successfully by faith! Consequently, you and I today must do the same!

~FAITH IS SPIRITUAL~

Faith is of a spiritual essence. It derives out of the person of God. **"GOD IS SPIRIT..."** (St. John 4:24) Faith is created by the Spirit of God within you. This transpires at the very moment of conception within your "spirit being." Faith is present in Gods character, and when he breathed into the nostrils of humankind the breath of life had within its essence faith from God!

~FAITH TESTED~

The measure of faith spoken of in the scriptures is an innate gift at birth. Every person has the capacity of faith which God has freely given for you to succeed in life. It does not mean that you don't have faith because you are going through some form of intense trial or pressure. Sometimes, you go through because you do have faith. Faith is often challenged by trial. How do you know what it can do if it is never challenged?

How do you know that your faith is weak or strong unless you are confronted with so called, "impossible situations?" A test is indeed faiths greatest measurement device!

You might ask the question, how do I know when my faith is working. As a general rule, you know that your faith is working when after giving the challenge or need over to God you become relaxed knowing that the need is now in good hands and whatever God decides to do, it is going to work our right for you. You see, God always know what, when and how to do. Your Heavenly Father has no nervous condition, he does not bite his fingernails, nor does he have to scratch his head to figure our how to solve our problems. So, if and when you place the situation in his hands why worry about it!

~DON'T SELF-DESTRUCT~

Never think that you don't have faith, because you're being assaulted by adversity. The adversity just might be a sign that you are on the right track. If adversity never comes your way beware you may be on the wrong track!

Daniel had faith and was put in a den of hungry lions! The Hebrew boys, Shadrach, Meshach, and

Abednego had faith, but were thrown in the midst of blazing fire! Jesus had faith but was hanged on a rugged cross! Even the New Testament church was born in the midst of intense persecution. Nevertheless, because of steadfast faith in the power of God the church survived!

You too, will survive the challenge necessary for reaching your God ordained potential if you refuse to self-destruct under antagonistic threat. Daniel's God is your God. Moses' God is your God. Paul's God is your God!

The bible declares that Jesus is the **"AUTHOR AND FINISHER OF OUR FAITH."** (Hebrews 12:2) So then, if this is true of which I have no doubt, how can I fail to reach and maximize my potential with my **"GOD KIND OF FAITH."** If and when I come into the Lords presence exercising the faith that Jesus is the "Author and Finisher" will God turn me away? No! Why? Because anytime I come into God's presence with authentic faith that Jesus is the author and finisher; God recognizes in me a reflection of himself, he views in me the faith of his Son Jesus. God will never turn Him away because their spirit is "one!"

God will never work against himself! So then my dear reader, you will succeed, you will overcome, you will fulfill your potential because you as a believer possess the **"GOD KIND OF FAITH!"**

~BE SELF CONFIDENT!

"Therefore do not cast away your confidence, which has great reward…" (Hebrews 10:35)

Confidence is that self-assurance that your faith is potent enough to produce visible and spiritual success. You have within your being the capacity of both valuable resources. Use them to their fullest value!

When an individual is constantly losing their confidence level is usually at a low degree. However, each victory over every challenge is a confidence builder. In times of defeat it is important that we maintain a degree of confidence. This degree of confidence is created by past success. These successes serve as a maintenance factor to your confidence level.

If you are to consummate your potential never loose confidence in yourself by throwing your faith away. Your faith working for you is predicated upon your own self-confidence and in the faith the Lord has allotted you. I believe there to be a thin line between confidence and faith.

Faith is present in you, but if you don's have confidence in it working for you, you can negatively victimize yourself. If no one believes in you, you ought to believe in you! Never form the opinion that God thinks more of someone else than he does you, and that someone else's faith is more valuable than yours.

The truth of the matter is all men are created in Gods image and he loves all with the same love. God loves you with the very life of His Son Jesus!

A gentleman once wrote me after listening to my weekly "Word of Life" radio broadcast. He was requesting my prayers of faith concerning a personal need in his life. I detected in the tone of his letter that he lacked self-confidence in his relationship with the Lord. While praying in regards to the gentlemen's request, I personally partitioned Gods guidance to give me how to respond back to the man in a written letter.

I wrote back expressing to the man how much God loved him. I also expressed to him how that the Lord would respond to him also if he would submit to Gods purpose and plan for his life. I further stated that he too, possessed favor with the Lord as much as I and that God would hear him when also prayed!

Maximizing one's potential requires much prayerful communication and faith for positive results. Always know that you have power and favor with the Lord and your faith in the personal relationship honors him and he in return honors you with his Divine Favor!

Persistence is a must when striving to be the best that you can be for the Masters glory. Never give up on yourself! As long as you have breath in your body, faith in your heart, and humility of spirit towards the Savior's will, you can achieve success!

~BE DETERMINED & PERSISTENT~

You have perhaps heard the proverb, 'Where there's a will there is a way." As a minister of the gospel of Jesus Christ I have found this wise saying to be very true. However, whether one's will develops into a living reality depends on his determination, and faith and persistence to achieve his goal, no matter what the price or sacrifice. There are many sincere Christians who have visions and dreams of doing bigger and better things for the cause of Christ in the earth but somehow somewhere along life's way they become discouraged by the challenge, thus allowing their faith to be weakened to the point of negatively effecting their persistence.

Never forget that if the purpose is noble and will bring glory to God you have a right to be persistent. Don't accept no for an answer! If the Lord is in the plan, work with the plan with all persistence and faithful commitment. Remember, you **"can do all things through Christ!"**

"The harder the thing is to do the greater the joy when it's done. The farther the goal is from you, the sweeter the thrill when it's won. The deeper the problem, the more is the joy when you've puzzled it out; the seas that run fartherest from shore are only for ships that are stout. Men weary of lessons they've learned and tire of the tasks they can do. Life, it seems is forever concerned with blazing a path to the new, so stand to the worry and care. Everlastingly, keep going on. The greater the burden, the greater the joy when it's done!"

Author Unknown

OMEGA

Lessons For Life

DAILY PRAYER PETITIONS

Thank you Father for allowing me the privilege to come into your presence. May this day be filled with your blessings upon my life so that I may be a blessing to others!

*****

Dear God I submit to your righteousness that your glory may be revealed and that those I walk among may be drawn to you because of what they see of you in me!

*****

Father God in the name of Jesus thank you for the incomparable beauty of your wonderful creation. May it always remind us that it is to your glory and our fortunate gift to enjoy!

*****

Father God in Jesus wonderful name forgive me for all offensive living to your righteousness, and may this moment in time find me walking in your righteousness in submission to your daily guidance!

*****

Lord I thank you for your peace that is within me that always abound over all antagonistic forces that come to rob me of your Divine joy that is within my spirit!

*****

Thank you Father for your faithfulness and abounding grace that embraces me on a daily basis!

*****

Dear God I submit to you my mind, body, and soul for your occupation and my daily confidence and comfort!

*****

Thank you Lord that your abounding blessings within my life far surpasses the negatives the evil adversary has utilized to try to defeat me!

*****

Dear Lord direct my path on a daily basis and may my walk with Christ always lead me through the difficulties I may encounter!

*****

Lord God in the name of Jesus may the words of my mouth and the meditation of my heart always reflect the light of your presence within my being!

*****

Lord I truly thank you for all the tough situations you have made it possible for me to overcome successfully. Your faithfulness is beyond measure and your grace is beyond comparison!

APPENDIX: "THOUGHTS TO PONDER"

The primary purpose of the church is to be the bride of Christ and bring forth children to enhance the family and Kingdom of God on the earth!

/////

God has already completed his act of salvation towards you. You must now accept that which He had done if it is to work for you!

/////

The ultimate gesture of God's salvation is consummated in the act of Jesus' death, burial, and resurrection. What more could He ever do to seal your salvation?

/////

The church does not have to immolate the world's style to attract people to accept Christ. Jesus alone is more than enough, emulate His lifestyle!

/////

Don't sell your relationship with God short. Always obey Him regardless of the difficulties and

you will be walking in His Divine Favor towards
unlimited success!

/////

Faith can be likened to "the currency of heaven."
According to your faith as you seek God's
blessings, heaven will respond appropriately!

/////

Self-pity blinds you to the reality of blessings you
already have in your possession. Stop dwelling on
the void and thank God for blessings past and
present!

/////

There are evil forces in the "spirit world" we are
all subject to confront. Your will to allow or
dismiss these influences from possessing you is
predicated in great measure upon your
acceptance or rejection of their invasion and
persuasion!

/////

The "heroes of faith" in Hebrews eleven were able
to be sustained in their experiences of trial

because they subjected themselves to be influenced by the "God kind of faith!"

/////

There is an inherent quality of Divine power you have been given by the Creator to control and determine your destiny!

/////

Satanic forces that are trying to control your life cannot defeat you unless you give them reason and bait to defeat you (i.e. fear, pity, doubt, etc.!)

/////

The peace of God within the believer defies the venomous darts of adversity that's intended to defeat your spiritual resolve to stay strong!

/////

Intelligence is relative to the subject matter you have thorough knowledge of and how well you are able to utilize it in a beneficial manner towards others as well as yourself!

/////

The moral fiber of humanity is in a state of decay. The gospel however, is more than qualified to rectify this rampant problem. The gospel contains the "Good News" powerful enough to bring deliverance to a sin inflicted soul!

/////

The Word of God must become more than written script if it is to work on your behalf. It will come alive within you as you act upon its precepts!

~NOTES~

_____
_____
_____
_____
_____
_____
_____
_____
_____
_____
_____
_____
_____
_____
_____
_____
_____
_____
_____
_____
_____
_____

_____
_____
_____
_____
_____
_____
_____
_____
_____
_____
_____
_____
_____
_____
_____
_____
_____
_____

ABOUT THE AUTHOR

At the age of eighteen, Eddie Jernagin accepted the Divine Call to minister and over the many years his powerful and practical words have been a blessing to countless thousands!

For 37 years, Dr. Eddie Jernagin pastured the Christ Is The Answer Church in Los Angeles, California. He is a noted Conference Speaker, Counselor, Bible Teacher, Adviser, International Radio Personality, Author and Bishop.

In 2012, he founded and is the president of **"New Dimensions International Ministries."** It's the evangelistic Bible Preaching and Teaching Ministry of Dr. Jernagin that's taking the Gospel of Jesus Christ unto the whole world.

Dr. Eddie Jernagin is a gifted writer of practical truth endeavoring to share vivid insights about life from a biblical perspective. He aspires to show how utilizing biblical principles as a guideline can provide righteous solutions for human kind to ultimately succeed beyond all negative obstacles.

Dr. Eddie Jernagin also serves as the Vice Prelate of the Governing Board and the Bishop of the Fourth Jurisdiction of The Convention Of Covenanting Churches.

His messages will inspire you to search the scriptures, study the Kingdom Principles of God, mature in your faith, listen and obey The Holy Spirit and walk in the victorious life that Christ has given you.

MORE AVAILABLE BOOKS BY
BISHOP EDDIE JERNAGIN

Man's Inheritance

Fulfilling Your Purpose

Communicating With God

Faith Building Exhortations

Opening The Door To A New Millennium

Wise Advice and Revelation Insights

The Blessing of Tough Experiences

Devising A Christian Marketing Strategy

MINISTRY CONTACT INFORMATION

Dr. Eddie Jernagin

New Dimension International Ministries

PO Box 976

MUNCIE, IN 47308

Website:

www.eddiejernagin.com

Email:

bishopeddiej@aol.com